T0065596

FROM ABOVE

Sherrill Eugene Stepter

WESTBOW
P R E S S°
A DIVISION OF THOMAS NELSON
& ZONDERVAN

Scripture taken from the Holy Bible, NEW INTERNATIONAL VERSION®.
Copyright © 1973, 1978, 1984, 2011 by Biblica, Inc. All rights reserved worldwide.
Used by permission. NEW INTERNATIONAL VERSION® and NIV® are
registered trademarks of Biblica, Inc. Use of either trademark for the offering
of goods or services requires the prior written consent of Biblica US, Inc.

WestBow Press books may be ordered through booksellers or by contacting:

WestBow Press
A Division of Thomas Nelson & Zondervan
1663 Liberty Drive
Bloomington, IN 47403
www.westbowpress.com
1 (866) 928-1240

Because of the dynamic nature of the Internet, any web addresses or
links contained in this book may have changed since publication and
may no longer be valid. The views expressed in this work are solely those
of the author and do not necessarily reflect the views of the publisher,
and the publisher hereby disclaims any responsibility for them.

Any people depicted in stock imagery provided by Thinkstock are models,
and such images are being used for illustrative purposes only.
Certain stock imagery © Thinkstock.

ISBN: 978-1-5127-5519-0 (sc)
ISBN: 978-1-5127-5520-6 (hc)
ISBN: 978-1-5127-5518-3 (e)

Library of Congress Control Number: 2016914353

Print information available on the last page.

WestBow Press rev. date: 08/31/2016

CONTENTS

PREFACE

I have always been fascinated by the fruit of the Spirit. The phrase implies tangible evidence that I can develop and grow the fruit of the Spirit in my life while I journey here on earth. Would this tangible evidence also validate my effort to become more like Christ in word and deed? In addition, would this goal provide a continual purpose and direction for each step I take?

These important questions require my ability to discern where I am presently in my walk with Christ as his follower in will and deed. Jesus is the way and the truth and the light and if I am a follower of Christ, I am on the right path. I believe that the fruit of the Spirit provides the ability to not only discern our present situation, but to provide the continual spiritual guidance as I grow as a follower of Christ in word and deed.

I am also enthralled by the nomenclature of the fruit of the Spirit. The fruit implies a singular idea or concept. Yet the list in Galatians 5:22–23 (New International Version) contains nine different elements. They come together to represent the same eternal unity that Jesus prays about in John 17:20–23.

"My prayer is not for them alone. I pray also for those who will believe in me through their message, that all of them may be one, Father, just as you are in me and I am in you. May they also be in us so that the world may believe that you have sent me. I have given them the glory that you gave me, that they may be one as we are one—I in them and you in me—so that they may be brought to complete unity. Then the world will know that you sent me and have loved them even as you have loved me."

Jesus was praying for all his followers to share the unity and love that he shares with God and the Holy Spirit. Even though Christ chose men from varied backgrounds and abilities, his goal was to unite them in presenting the gospel to the whole world. That is his goal for us as well.

In my pursuit, I have read and studied many books and online articles on the fruit of the Spirit. I have listened to many recorded talks on this subject as well. I have also invested many hours in the study of God's word while examining each of the nine traits. I developed an adult Bible class on the fruit of the Spirit and spent many hours in prayer before preparing and delivering each lesson. From the very beginning of my endeavor, I prayed over all my studies that the Holy Spirit would work through me or around me when I got in the way.

Early on a Sunday morning, as I was praying, God revealed that the lesson and handouts for the morning class needed serious tweaking. This tweaking was very lengthy, and I was concerned about being ready for the Sunday morning class. The lesson, after tweaking, was much better, and I was grateful for the divine guidance.

I loved sharing the fruit of the Spirit in the classes that I taught, but I was not satisfied that all this research and information should remain buried in one of my computers or in the portable backup system I carry with me all the time. So I decided to take the plunge and publish this work.

It was not easy to find a publisher for this book. The Lord led me to WestBow Press. With my publisher's assistance, this novice writer's book has been readied for publication. The technical side of book publication is as complicated as writing—almost as detailed and demanding.

Finally, I have a suggestion when you are studying each individual element of the fruit of the Spirit: Read and study each of these chapters on separate days or over longer periods of time. There was some concern about student overload when I was teaching one element weekly to an adult class.

I have provided a list of scriptural references from each of these chapters for information separate from the specific text. I have also provided a list of citations for the quotes from BrainyQuote.com.

In addition, you may wish to use other versions of the Bible to enrich your study. All scriptural material in this book was taken from the New International Version (NIV) Holy Bible, New International Version®, NIV® Copyright ©1973, 1978, 1984, 2011 by <u>Biblica, Inc.</u>® Used by permission. All rights reserved worldwide. My prayer is that this book will be of lasting value to you and will assist you in your short journey on earth. Thank you very much for reading this preface.

CHAPTER 1

Introduction

I had the privilege of teaching a week-long technical class on computer programming at a large corporation in Houston, Texas, back in the 1990s. Between the teaching, the labs, and the evening preparation for the next day, I was getting very tired. After lunch one day, I was exiting the restroom and suddenly realized that I did not recognize anything and did not know where I was. I was disoriented and scared. What a horrible feeling! I honestly had no clue as to my whereabouts. Fortunately the incident only lasted a few seconds. Being totally disoriented was unnerving, to say the least. Losing our way spiritually may not be as subtle, but it can be just as overwhelming when we realize we have wandered away. The consequences of being spiritually lost for any length of time can be our undoing—both now and forever.

The gooney birds of Midway Island are hilarious to watch as they land and take off.

When they land too fast, their crashes are fun to observe. Sometimes their high-speed landings end in tumbling over and over. On many attempted takeoffs, they may not choose a long and clear runway and may end up running into each other, into trees, or other stationary objects. Sometimes they literally run into the sea while attempting to take flight. Fortunately they are resilient. They keep on trying until they achieve flight.

The wingspan of a gooney bird can be greater than twelve feet, and a young gooney bird must spend hours and hours developing the wing muscles to support this span. Without flight, the gooney bird cannot survive. But once in the air, there is a dramatic change. The gooney bird suddenly transforms into an albatross when in the air. Albatrosses are arguably the masters of soaring. With their enormous wingspans and natural abilities, they can soar for hours and travel great distances.

Albatrosses have been known to fly hundreds of miles in a single round trip to find food for themselves and their offspring. When landing, taking off, or engaging in other activities on land, the albatross can quickly transform back into a gooney bird.

Albatrosses have many admirable qualities, but they are at their best when they soar on the winds that God provides. Midway Island, which is a natural habitat for gooney birds, is hundreds of miles from other landmasses and is quite small in comparison to Hawaii. Once airborne, an albatross must maintain his or her sense of location and direction at all times when flying long distances over the ocean. God has provided a natural positioning system for the albatross to make these arduous, repeated journeys both safely and successfully time after time. Has God provided a spiritual positioning system for followers, especially when they need a spiritual compass? This guidance system, better known as the fruit of the Spirit, is the GPS from above. I use that acronym, GPS, for God's powerful Spirit. So the book is named GPS from Above.

I am a spiritual soul on an eternal quest to be with God, but the earthly part of my journey continues to make me worldly. I transform into a spiritual being and soar in God's grace and mercy as the power of the Holy Spirit lifts me higher and higher. Sometimes I can almost touch heaven while singing, praying, and reading the Bible. I truly believe that all followers of Christ can almost touch heaven at times while here on earth. Yet I continue to lose my way. What transforms me back into being a worldly person? I want to continually soar in faith and yet I lose my direction and purpose repeatedly. Why?

John warns us in 1 John 2:16: "For everything in the world—the lust of the flesh, the lust of the eyes, and the pride of life—comes not from the Father but from the world." As John wrote, Satan forces his way into my thoughts through the lust of the flesh, the lust of the eye, or the pride of my heart. Then I am transformed once again into an earthly being foolishly pursuing earthly trappings—and I resemble a gooney bird at times. Is this what I really want? Are these earthly trappings really that important or necessary? Is my mind so polluted with earthly thoughts that I am facing spiritual starvation or even spiritual death? Am I the only one who feels like this?

Fortunately I can change my thoughts and replace them with biblically inspired thoughts. I am made in the image of God, and God does have an eternal plan for me. Is there a GPS from above for every follower of Christ?

In Luke 12:6 we read, "Are not five sparrows sold for two pennies? Yet not one of them is forgotten by God." From the tiny sparrow to the albatross with its twelve-foot wingspan, no creature is forgotten by God. God remembers and keeps a watchful eye over all his creations. Did you know that the symbolic all-seeing eye, on the top of a pyramid, is engraved on the back of the dollar bill? I choose to believe this symbol represents God's all-seeing eye as he watches over our nation.

Is God keeping a watchful eye over me? God's promises are endless for all followers of Christ. Yet I sometimes feel that the needle (Jesus Christ) has fallen out of my spiritual compass and that I am not surrendering my life in obedience to God. Worse, I feel as if I have lost my sense of direction and purpose from time to time. Do you feel this way at times?

If God has provided a natural positioning system for all the creatures on earth, can I assume that, since I am made in his image, I have a godly positioning system through God's powerful Spirit for my eternal soul—GPS from above? John 14:6 tells us, "Jesus answered, 'I am the way and the truth and the life. No one comes to the Father except through me.'"

My heart is beating faster as I try to fully grasp that Jesus is indeed the way, the truth, and the life, and through Jesus I can come to God. Yes, I am continually in the sight of God, and God has provided a spiritual positioning system to make my arduous journey on earth filled with both safety and certainty time and time again. With Jesus as the needle in my spiritual compass, with the Holy Spirit dwelling in me, and with God's word, I can stay the course.

If I am to recover and maintain my spiritual direction and purpose, what do I need to do today to keep on going forward in Christ? Is it plausible that our thoughts eventually lead to our words, our words eventually lead to our actions, and our actions eventually become our habits? Is it also plausible that our habits eventually shape our character and that our character eventually become our destiny? It sounds very reasonable and believable that our thoughts are so critical to our spiritual well being.

Wow! My thoughts lead to my words, which lead to my actions. Those actions lead to my habits, which lead to my character, and my character leads to my destiny. If this logical flow has validity, my thoughts would be a good place to start so that I can have a better life in Christ today and tomorrow. Life in Christ implies—or, better yet, demands—that Christ be the needle in my spiritual compass and that being a follower should fill my thoughts, my words, my deeds, and my very soul.

So how do I grow the eternal fruit to fuel my thoughts— thoughts that should eventually help me become more like

Christ in word and deed? Thank you, heavenly Father, for Galatians 5:22–23 and its list of the fruit of the Spirit that can grow in the hearts of your followers and enable us to develop and mature fully. Thank you for your precious word, your gift of the Holy Spirit, and for your only begotten Son! In Jesus' name, amen!

God has provided GPS from above to help me locate and eventually find my way to heaven.

In John 1:46, Philip gives the perfect response to a very important question.

"'Nazareth! Can anything good come from there?' Nathanael asked. 'Come and see,' said Philip."

Please travel with me in this study and 'come and see' for yourself. Please make GPS from Above part of your journey on earth and pray for both of us!

CHAPTER 2
Where Do I Begin?

In John 14:6, we read, "Jesus answered, 'I am the way and the truth and the life. No one comes to the Father except through me.'" I want to be a follower of Christ because of this statement. There is no alternative for those who want to come to our heavenly Father. Until I fully realize and live by this scripture, it will be very difficult for streams of living water to flow through me to others. There is no greater task. There is no higher calling. So where do I begin?

In John 14:16–17, Jesus promises, "And I will ask the Father, and he will give you another advocate to help you and be with you forever—the Spirit of truth. The world cannot accept him, because it neither sees him nor knows him. But you know him, for he lives with you and will be in you."

In John 14:23, we find more good news: "Jesus replied, 'Anyone who loves me will obey my teaching. My Father will love them, and we will come to them and make our home with them.'" Truly John 14 is a comforting chapter for all followers. I must continually read and study God's living word for understanding and guidance. Certainly John 14 may be a good text to start one's journey using the GPS from above! The entire book of John is certainly important for every follower to read and study.

Another blessing is found in Psalm 119:105: "Your word is a lamp for my feet, a light on my path." In other words, I must read and study for myself—not only God's word, but other inspired books as well. We are so blessed because we have God's living word in many translations and versions. Through the Internet, virtually anywhere we travel, we also have access to God's living word in electronic form within reach of our fingertips. God's living word is there for all of us to read and study and learn of God's great love for all of us. We can read and study God's word in almost any language or format. We are so blessed!

However, it is still my responsibility to open God's living word and make it my travel guide while here on earth. I am the only one who is responsible for my knowledge, for my understanding of God's living word, and for letting it direct my life. I am the only one who will answer to God on the Day of Judgment for my journey on earth as a follower not just a believer. Inside God's living word is where I must begin. I am seeking the GPS from above in his word with the help of the Holy Spirit.

Even Paul was not proud of his post conversion behavior as he wrote of his personal struggles in Romans 7:14–15: "We know that the law is spiritual; but I am unspiritual, sold as a slave to sin. I do not understand what I do. For what I want to do I do not do, but what I hate I do." Paul was puzzled with the reality that he was constantly in a worldly struggle as a follower. If Paul was vulnerable, I am certainly in big trouble! Yes, so are you! All the names of the followers of Christ stay on Satan's hit list.

Fortunately Paul wrote about life through the Holy Spirit in Romans 8. Paul wrote about those who may live in the earthly realm but journey with God in the heavenly realm. I am on an eternal spiritual journey, but right now I am on a temporary, earthly journey as well. As I travel here, sometimes I resemble a gooney bird when I let earthly things overwhelm my thoughts. But sometimes I am an albatross, and the Holy Spirit lifts me up from earthly concerns to heavenly realms with thoughts of eternity with God. Singing praises to God works for me as well. Oh, how I love to sing!

Paul provided additional insight in Titus 3:4–7: "But when the kindness and love of God our Savior appeared, he saved us, not because of righteous things we had done, but because of his mercy. He saved us through the washing of rebirth and renewal by the Holy Spirit, whom he poured out on us generously through Jesus Christ our Savior, so that, having been justified by his grace, we might become heirs having the hope of eternal life."

I need to read this text over and over, or perhaps I should put it in a prominent place to refresh my thoughts and renew my commitment to follow Christ. I love the word *renewal* in verse five because my Savior promises to be there for me regardless of my current situation. He is always there for me!

The purpose of the Spirit's presence in the heart and life of a follower is to become more and more like Christ. I must continually renew my efforts to be like Christ in my thoughts, words, deeds, habits, character, and life. This is the purpose for which I must strive. I most certainly have an obligation to the Holy Spirit that is living in me. I cannot change yesterday; I can only prepare for tomorrow. I can, however, do what must be done today!

CHAPTER 3

What Must I Do Today?

I believe that eternal truths are only found in the word of God. In the latter part of Galatians 5, Paul writes about life in the Spirit. If the Holy Spirit is our advocate and a critical part of our GPS from above, then perhaps we can find what we must do today as we read and study the truths in Galatians 5. Paul compares life in the flesh and life in the Spirit—the struggle that every one of us continually faces.

In addition, Jesus addresses the internal struggle everyone faces in Matthew 15:18–19: "But the things that come out of a person's mouth come from the heart, and these defile them. For out of the heart come evil thoughts—murder, adultery, sexual immorality, theft, false testimony, slander."

The struggle begins in our thoughts and shows the outcome in our words and deeds. Can you imagine the struggle Peter had on the night that he betrayed Christ three times? Is it possible that I, like Peter, deny Christ at times? We know the answer to that question. I have an ongoing struggle to keep Christ in every facet of my life—to strengthen me, guide me, and protect me—for Jesus is the way, the truth, and the life.

Here are some interesting quotes about thoughts, words, and deeds.

> As a single footstep will not make a path on the earth, so a single thought will not make a pathway in the mind. To make a deep physical path, we walk again and again. To make a deep mental path, we must think over and over the kind of thoughts we wish to dominate our lives. (Henry David Thoreau)[1]

> Who you are speaks so loudly I can't hear what you're saying. (Ralph Waldo Emerson)[2]

> It is in our lives and not our words that our religion must be read. (Thomas Jefferson)[3]

Paul writes about the fruit of the Spirit—the growing effect of the advocate that enables us to become more and more like Christ. In Galatians 5:22–23, it is recorded, "But the fruit of the Spirit is love, joy, peace, forbearance, kindness, goodness, faithfulness, gentleness and self-control. Against such things there is no law."

Paul also writes about life without the Spirit—the sinful nature that is in continual conflict with the Spirit. In Galatians 5:19–21 we read, "The acts of the flesh are obvious: sexual immorality, impurity and debauchery; idolatry and witchcraft; hatred, discord, jealousy, fits of rage, selfish ambition, dissensions, factions and envy; drunkenness, orgies, and the like. I warn you, as I did before, that those who live like this will not inherit the kingdom of God."

In these five verses of Galatians 5 are listed the acts of the flesh and the fruit of the Spirit for the soul. These five verses list two different lifestyles—one that gratifies the longing of the flesh and one that gratifies the longing of the soul. If my thoughts eventually form my character, then what thoughts currently occupy my mind? What thoughts should I allow to occupy my mind?

Warning: no commitment is too big when it is for someone else. I must personalize my own commitment and let others do the same. I have an eternal commitment that is impossible to achieve. But with the advocate of the GPS from above, the Holy Spirit living in me, all things are possible. I can do this because Jesus Christ leads the way, and I am a follower even though I am a work in progress. God, please hold me in the palm of your hand forever! In Jesus' name, amen!

This is as personal as it gets. I must carefully examine each of these elements of the fruit of the Spirit to find ways to restore and renew my direction and purpose daily. This will require a lot of reading and study. So before we begin, let's start with a quick review.

Romans 8:1–2 tells us, "Therefore, there is now no condemnation for those who are in Christ Jesus, because through Christ Jesus the law of the Spirit who gives life has set you free from the law of sin and death." Remember, Jesus was completely perfect and was never under the power of sin, yet his will was always the will of his Father and our God. If we are true followers of Christ, we are indeed free from the law of sin and death, but our will must align with the will of God. Jesus Christ has to be the needle in our spiritual compass.

Paul goes into great detail in Chapter 8 on being a follower and the reasons why. The bottom line is that one choice leads to death and one choice leads to life and peace. Remember, the consequences of sin can take away everything and everyone you hold dear—now and forever. Oh, what a terrible price to pay! The simple choice is follow the path to eternal life by being a follower of Christ.

Almost all communication is nonverbal, so our actions must be ongoing examples of Christ living in us. Even though we are free in Christ Jesus, we must show our faith by our actions. Our words and our actions must be in harmony with our beliefs as followers. I would much rather witness a sermon than hear a sermon any time. The best example is to show Christ to others in deeds that display the fruit of the Spirit.

I purpose that my life of being a follower of can be measured by the fruit of the Spirit in my life. If I am growing and developing the fruit of the Spirit and following the commands of Christ, I am certainly emulating Christ in my life and making him the needle in my spiritual compass. Thus I am traveling on God's highway with the GPS from above as my navigator.

I have two choices, and the first choice is to live according to the inclinations of the flesh. My second choice is to be on the earth but not worldly. We are children of God and heirs to eternity in heaven. So we must be followers and determined to develop the fruit of the Spirit.

We are indeed free from the law of sin and death, but we also have a higher calling: to be true followers of Christ in all our ways. I must decide to choose Christ again and again as the needle in my spiritual compass and accept my purpose: becoming more like Christ as I journey here on earth. I have to read and study God's word and I will need heavenly help. I will need lots of time with God in prayer and the indwelling of the Holy Spirit. I will need the GPS from above for this goal. I must truly add direction and obedience to my desire to become more like Christ.

We are going to look at each element of the fruit of the Spirit in depth and turn this knowledge into active wisdom by applying it directly in our lives. God will provide, and Jesus has sent his advocate, so let's begin our endeavor with prayer.

Loving heavenly Father, I am asking to accomplish the seemingly impossible task of becoming more like your son daily. I cannot do it without your love, grace, and mercy. Please give me ears not only to hear but to listen. Please give me eyes not only to look but to see. Please give me hands not only to feel but to grasp your word and never let go. Please give me a mouth not only to speak but to reveal my love for you and my love for all your children. Please give me a heart not only to love but to grow in your wisdom and understanding. Please, may I become more like your Son daily and truly be a follower all the days of my life. In Jesus' name, amen!

God bless you and yours as we begin to tweak (recalculate) our journey on earth with the GPS from above, using Galatians 5:22–23 as our reference.

CHAPTER 4

GPS of Love

In Galatians 5:22–23, we read, "But the fruit of the Spirit is love, joy, peace, forbearance, kindness, goodness, faithfulness, gentleness and self-control. Against such things there is no law."

The purpose of the Holy Spirit's presence in the heart and life of a follower of Christ is to help us grow and mature and soar on wings of faith. We must continue to renew our efforts to be more like Christ in thought, in words, in deeds, in habits, in character, and in life.

Why does the fruit of the Spirit begin with love?

In a conversation recorded in the latter part of Matthew 22, Jesus was questioned about the greatest commandment of all. His answers are found in Matthew 22:37–39: "Jesus replied: 'Love the Lord your God with all your heart and with all your soul and with all your mind. This is the first and greatest commandment. And the second is like it: Love your neighbor as yourself.'"

Please do not overlook "as yourself." God wants me to love myself and build a good foundation for loving others. How can I possibly love others as I should when I do not love myself as I should? Our Heavenly Father loves us beyond our ability to know or comprehend. Oh heavenly Father, help us to appreciate truly that we are made in your image, that we are your children, and that you love us beyond measure. In Jesus' name, amen!

With regard to loving my neighbor as myself, there is a reality about myself that I must face as well. If I understand this commandment correctly, I need to be on very loving terms with myself and accept the fact that I have been my own worst enemy at times. I lose my way so many times by not letting Christ be the needle in my spiritual compass. I need to understand fully that I am a struggling Christian and that God loves me as I am at this moment in my journey. However, God wants more for me and from me! What loving parents do not want more for their children and from their children?

Here are some interesting quotes about love.

> Being deeply loved by someone gives you strength; loving someone deeply gives you courage. (Lao Tzo)[4]

> Lord, grant that I might not so much seek to be loved as to love. (Saint Francis of Assisi)[5]

Keep love in your heart. A life without it is like a sunless garden when the flowers are dead. (Oscar Wilde)[6]

In English, we have one word for love. The Greeks had at least four.

- *eros*: desire toward some person or thing
- *philia*: friendship love
- *storge*: natural affection for those closest to us
- *agape*: selfless love, supernatural love, divinely powered

How do I personally define love? Now is a good time to write down how you and I define love. Please take a moment and write your definition. Thank you!

_____

_____

_____

Without a doubt, the Bible is a perfect place to search for and define love. The Bible allows us to understand its importance and the fruit it can produce in our lives. In Colossians 3:14 we read, "And over all these virtues put on love, which binds them all together in perfect unity." Love helps bring true meaning to the other elements of the fruit of the Spirit and helps us truly bring all these elements of the fruit of the Spirit together to perfection.

Love is fully *agape* only when that love directs all we do as followers, not just as believers. Even Satan believes that Jesus Christ is the Son of God. In 1 Corinthians 13:1–3, it is written, "If I speak in the tongues of men or of angels, but do not have love, I am only a resounding gong or a clanging cymbal. If I have the gift of prophecy and can fathom all mysteries and all knowledge, and if I have a faith that can move mountains, but do not have love, I am nothing. If I give all I possess to the poor and give over my body to hardship that I may boast, but do not have love, I gain nothing." Regardless of what we say and do for Christ and for others, our words and actions are meaningless without love.

Love is defined by the Spirit through Paul in 1 Corinthians 13:4–8a: "Love is patient, love is kind. It does not envy, it does not boast, it is not proud. It does not dishonor others, it is not self-seeking, it is not easily angered, it keeps no record of wrongs. Love does not delight in evil but rejoices with the truth. It always protects, always trusts, always hopes, always perseveres. Love never fails." These verses specify what love is, why it is so important, and how it can be measured daily in my life.

How did I show my love for myself and others today? Was I terrible in traffic? Was I rude? Was I envious? I can go on and on—but enough about me. If I rated my acts of love today, how did I do? These acts of love should be viewed as "under construction" to help me realize that God is not finished with me yet. Perfection is a wonderful goal, but performance of loving acts, whether perfect or not, is really necessary. I am on the earthly part of my eternal journey, and God's powerful spirit is very active in me if I follow Christ. God will not let me down, and the Holy Spirit is eternally perfect and powerful. The only flaw in all of this is my allowing Satan to deter me. I must remember that I am a work in progress. I can learn and do better. God will provide.

Everyone needs more love in their lives. Sometimes those who need love the most deserve it the least. Love is easier and lighter than hate to carry in my heart. So I must choose love in every situation. I am grateful for my wife and her endless capacity to show love for everyone, especially me.

Love is the very essence of our lives. It is the foundation for today and eternity. In John 3:16, we can read about the greatest gift of love: "For God so loved the world that he gave his one and only Son, that whoever believes in him shall not perish but have eternal life." This gift tells us how much God truly loves us—yes, even when we least deserve love.

Now I need to begin putting more love in my life for others and for myself immediately. (Remember that command to love others "as yourself.") Perhaps a very practical homework assignment is just what I need. I hate to do homework alone. Join me!

Homework

Three Simple Rules for Today

1) Do nothing hurtful to anyone. Show *agape* for everyone, including yourself. Luke 6:31 reads, "Do to others as you would have them do to you."

2) Do good everywhere you can, showing love in action. Matthew 5:43–45a reads, "You have heard that it was said, 'Love your neighbor and hate your enemy.' But I tell you, love your enemies and pray for those who persecute you, that you may be children of your Father in heaven." Good deeds do not go unnoticed and continue to ripple through so many lives like waves upon the ocean.

3) Continually grow your love for God. His promises alone show why we should increase our love for God. In Matthew 5:3–10 are many sacred promises that explain how we are blessed. The poor in spirit receive the kingdom of heaven. The mourners receive comfort. The meek inherit the earth. Those who are starving spiritually are filled with the living water. The merciful receive mercy. The pure in heart shall see God. The peacemakers become children of God. Those who are persecuted in Christ receive the kingdom of heaven. These promises are why we should continually seek God in his word and in prayer and fall more deeply in love with God daily.

I must not say or do harmful things to others or myself continually. I must be good and do good deeds at every opportunity. I will cherish the stream of living water that will flow to and through me as I share God's love for others and myself.

God will provide the growth in others and in me! I will talk to God more in prayer, and I will listen to God more in my heart. I have one mouth, two ears, and two eyes, so I should spend much more time listening and observing and less time talking. This is really tough for me; I do love to talk. I can hear those who know me saying, "Amen."

In serenity, I must spend more time observing how God shows his love in my life, family, church family, work family, and neighborhood. Thank you, heavenly Father, for your endless and eternal love. In Jesus' name, amen!

The fruit of the Spirit is love!

CHAPTER 5

GPS of Joy

As we have read in Galatians 5:22–23, "But the fruit of the Spirit is love, joy, peace, forbearance, kindness, goodness, faithfulness, gentleness and self-control. Against such things there is no law."

The purpose of the Holy Spirit's presence in the heart and life of a follower of Christ is to help us grow and mature and soar on wings of faith. We must continue to renew our efforts to be more like Christ in thought, in words, in deeds, in habits, in character, and in life.

In Hebrews 3:1, we read, "Therefore, holy brothers and sisters, who share in the heavenly calling, fix your thoughts on Jesus, whom we acknowledge as our apostle and high priest." We are to focus on Jesus by making him the needle in our spiritual compass. We must never assume we are always on the right path.

Have you ever known anyone who has never been discouraged? Why is it that some people rebound resiliently despite their circumstances? It is so important to be surrounded by people who help us to grow and mature joyfully in Christ. To whom would you turn when you need encouragement? Why?

Here is a more heavenly definition of joy. Joy is the positive confidence we feel from knowing and trusting God regardless of circumstances. This is not a temporary condition but an ongoing understanding that God is in control. This condition is not an option.

Here are some unique quotes about joy.

> When you rise in the morning, give thanks for the light, for your life, for your strength. Give thanks for your food and for the joy of living. If you see no reason to give thanks, the fault lies in yourself. (Tecumseh)[7]

> Friendship improves happiness and abates misery, by the doubling of our joy and the dividing of our grief.
> (Marcus Tullius Cicero)[8]

> Tears of joy are like the summer rain drops pierced by sunbeams. (Hosea Ballou)[9]

Where do my choices fit into my walk with God? How am I choosing to use his GPS from above to increase my joy? God has given me the ability to make wise choices. So which should I choose?

- Am I sharing joy or misery?
- Am I smiling or scowling?
- Am I grateful or hateful?
- Am I looking up or down?

Pain and suffering are inevitable, but misery is a choice. If misery is optional, why would I choose misery, scowling, being hateful, or being down? Ouch! This exploration of joy is going from being friendly to meddling. How do people really see me? Satan is the only one who gains when I relive my failures and put myself down.

Choices impact our joy enormously. So I need to examine choices I have made and continue to make. Many choices surround me: friends, spouse, work, church, reading, entertainment, and my time with God.

Do my friends lift me up or tear me down? Can there be an element of truth in a putdown? I must choose friends who lift me up, and I need to be grateful for those wonderful friends. Am I a blessing to my friends? Who has too many true friends?

Does my spouse make me a better person? Marriage is a work in progress, and I can tell you, even after forty-seven years of marriage, that a marriage takes commitment to each other. I must choose to commit. I must truly love and honor the person who chose to walk hand in hand with me and who brings me continual joy.

Does my work bring me joy? I must choose to commit my work to God and create a work environment that produces joy in me. I must share that joy.

Does my church help me to grow more and more in love with God? I must help my church to do this. I must look for ways to spread joy, especially to my brothers and sisters in Christ.

What do I read? Reading directly impacts my thoughts. Garbage in, garbage out! Again, hate what is evil and cling to what is good. Currently I am reading about the founding fathers and how the Constitution and Bill of Rights were created. Some of the information is very detailed and enlightening. I am trying to discover and understand the beginning purposes and assess how we are doing as a nation now.

What entertainment do I enjoy? It must make me laugh and not be too serious. I need to laugh a lot—the personal health benefits are endless. I also must filter what I watch because it will affect my sleep. Shows are rated now because not all of their material is suitable for our children and for children of God. In Romans 12:9 we read that "love must be sincere. Hate what is evil; cling to what is good." I must be very careful of what I allow to enter my mind. If you are what you eat, then it makes sense that you are what you consume mentally. I love sight gags (visual jokes) and need closed captions to enjoy entertainment. I can hardly wait for movies to come out on

DVD so I can turn on closed captions and find out what I missed. I joyfully discovered that closed caption is offered at movie theatres using a device that you place in the cup holder. You have to ask for the device, but it's free.

Is my time with God helping me love God more and more? I choose to pray, meditate on his word, involve him in all my decisions, and show an example of living water flowing through me to the world. How am I doing with this effort? Not very well, but these are great choices, and following Christ is such a worthy endeavor. God wants me to be perfect, but God loves me deeply anyway.

There is one more obstacle to joy that you and I must face.

That barrier is the incomplete sentence that begins, "I will be happy as soon as I …"

Fortunately for safety and sight, a motor vehicle's rear-view mirror is much smaller than the windshield. Even with the use of side-view mirrors, the view ahead is much larger and clearer. Can we see a spiritual lesson in this? We need to see joy for what it really is! We can lose the joy of today if we spend too much time looking back at yesterday.

Joy is not a lingering feeling. It is a choice I choose to make. Joy is not based upon circumstances but upon my attitude and my faith. It is free to all, but it is not cheap. It is one element of the fruit of the Spirit and of a growing relationship with Jesus Christ. I need to realize that I must choose to see and live a joyous life with help from the GPS from above. Here are a few tips from God's word about joyful living.

Joy is diminished because of:

- Selfishness and envy diminish joy. In James 3:16 is written, "For where you have envy and selfish ambition, there you find disorder and every evil practice."
- Bitterness also diminishes joy. In Hebrews 12:15 we read, "See to it that no one falls short of the grace of God and that no bitter root grows up to cause trouble and defile many."
- Fear, too, diminishes joy. In 1 John 4:18a, we read, "There is no fear in love. But perfect love drives out fear, because fear has to do with punishment."

Joy can expand because of"

- Giving increases joy. Acts 20:35 reads, "In everything I did, I showed you that by this kind of hard work we must help the weak, remembering the words the Lord Jesus himself said: 'It is more blessed to give than to receive.'"
- Remembrance also increases joy. In John 3:16, we read, "For God so loved the world that he gave his one and only Son, that whoever believes in him shall not perish but have eternal life."
- Joy also increases through healing rather than hurting. Colossians 3:13 instructs us, "Bear with each other and

forgive one another if any of you has a grievance against someone. Forgive as the Lord forgave you."

- We gain joy through our trust in God. Psalms 62:8 reads, "Trust in him at all times, you people; pour out your hearts to him, for God is our refuge."

What is the central theme of Philippians? The words for *joy*, *rejoice*, and *gladness* appear fifteen times in its 104 verses. Joy is the positive confidence we feel from knowing and trusting God regardless of the circumstances.

Philippians 4:4 reads, "Rejoice in the Lord always. I will say it again: Rejoice!" Joy is a choice.

Philippians 4:13 reads, "I can do all this through him who gives me strength." We must learn to rely on God always!

Again, joy is the positive confidence we feel from knowing and trusting God regardless of the circumstances. I can choose to increase my joy this week. There is not enough joy in your world or mine. Help me increase the joy.

The fruit of the Spirit is joy!

CHAPTER 6

GPS of Peace

Let us return to Galatians 5:22–23, which tells us, "But the fruit of the Spirit is love, joy, peace, forbearance, kindness, goodness, faithfulness, gentleness and self-control. Against such things there is no law."

The purpose of the Holy Spirit's presence in the heart and life of a follower of Christ is to help us grow and mature and soar on wings of faith. We must continue to renew our efforts to be more like Christ in thought, in words, in deeds, in habits, in character, and in life.

I cannot remember a time when the world was at peace. In 1 John 2:16, John warns us that Satan will force his way into our thoughts through the lust of the flesh, the lust of the eye, and the pride of the heart. The lack of world peace and the fact that our Constitution has a Bill of Rights to ensure individual protection from our own government both attest that the devil is very active today. Also, in 1 Peter 5:8, it is written, "Be alert and of sober mind. Your enemy the devil prowls around like a roaring lion looking for someone to devour."

The devil is texting evil thoughts to my mind continually to disturb my inner peace and fill me with worries, regret, and doubt. Although I have lived many years, I fall victim to the devil's efforts time and time again. The devil has been tempting humans for thousands of years. He is very powerful and can disrupt my peace at any time if I am not prepared.

Fortunately I am not responsible for world peace, but I am responsible for my personal peace. Can I truly bring peace to others when I am not at peace with myself? I believe that the desire for peace is universal. However, there are so many times when I am not at peace over worldly concerns. Lord, help me to minimize those times and follow your example on my journey.

What can make peace go away? The list of disruptions is almost endless, and many of these are real and valid. Personal peace can be disrupted from without and within. I need to examine possible areas in my life that can be tweaked to help me keep internal peace. I need to find a way to be a peaceful influence wherever I am.

What are my real wants and needs? Do my priorities really reflect what is important to me? Does my daily schedule reflect what is really important to me? Enough already—let me see how this past week was spent and what took my energy and time. Perhaps this review will reveal one or more flaws in how I invest my time and help me understand why peace can suddenly disappear.

This may be a good opportunity for you as well! Please log your activity just for one day. You might be surprised! Ask your spouse about your time and priorities! If you want a special treat, ask your teenagers too.

How much devotional time did I give to God this week? How much time did I give to my family? How much time do I spend eating and sleeping? How much time was dedicated to getting ready for work, the commute to and from work, and working at the office? How much work (physical and mental) do I bring home? Let me dare not forget the greatest time robbers of all—electronic devices.

Okay! After I review how I have invested my time and energy and listed my activities, what does this imply? After reviewing all the data, what would I do differently to increase peace in my life? Perhaps you can profit from this exercise as well.

What are some concerns that should <u>not</u> disturb our peace?

We are concerned about physical wants and needs. Matthew 6:31–32 reads, "So do not worry, saying, 'What shall we eat?' or 'What shall we drink?' or 'What shall we wear?' For the pagans run after all these things, and your heavenly Father knows that you need them."

We are concerned about so many areas in our lives that we have absolutely no control, yet we continue to worry. In John 16:33, we read, "I have told you these things, so that in me you may have peace. In this world you will have trouble. But take heart! I have overcome the world."

We are overwhelmed by too many problems. In John 14:27, we read, "Peace I leave with you; my peace I give you. I do not give to you as the world gives. Do not let your hearts be troubled and do not be afraid."

We are concerned over so many non-eternal issues. Luke 10:41–42 mentions such concerns. "'Martha, Martha,' the Lord answered, 'you are worried and upset about many things, but few things are needed—or indeed only one. Mary has chosen what is better, and it will not be taken away from her.'" Lord take control, please!

What are some types of peace that we should seek?

Spiritual peace—we desire reconciliation with God, which results in compatibility with God. Spiritual peace is emphasized in Romans 5:1: "Therefore, since we have been justified through faith, we have peace with God through our Lord Jesus Christ."

It is also highlighted in Colossians 1:20: "And through him to reconcile to himself all things, whether things on earth or things in heaven, by making peace through his blood, shed on the cross."

Personal peace—we all want to be at peace with God. Colossians 3:15a reminds us, "Let the peace of Christ rule in your hearts, since as members of one body you were called to peace."

Philippians 4:6–7 helps us focus. There we read, "Do not be anxious about anything, but in every situation, by prayer and petition, with thanksgiving, present your requests to God. And the peace of God, which transcends all understanding, will guard your hearts and your minds in Christ Jesus." This promise provides reconciliation with God.

<u>Relational peace</u>—No one wants enemies. I have found that the more I speak, the more likely I am to make an enemy. Relational peace is reconciliation with others whenever and wherever you have the opportunity. Romans 12:18 urges us to reconcile with others: "If it is possible, as far as it depends on you, live at peace with everyone." Hebrews 12:14 has similar instructions: "Make every effort to live in peace with everyone and to be holy; without holiness no one will see the Lord."

To be an albatross and soar in peace, I need to follow the directions in Ephesians 4:3—"Make every effort to keep the unity of the Spirit through the bond of peace." But how do I do this?

1. Take the initiative—"Go at once and make peace," as in Matthew 5:24.
2. Empathize with others—remove your barriers and don't attack theirs.
3. Focus on the issue, not the individual—say no harmful words.
4. Be flexible—be willing to yield to others.
5. Make reconciliation, rather than resolution, your goal, as urged in 2 Corinthians 5:18: "All this is from God,

who reconciled us to himself through Christ and gave us the ministry of reconciliation."

In 1 Peter 3:10–12, we read, "For, 'Whoever would love life and see good days must keep their tongue from evil and their lips from deceitful speech. They must turn from evil and do good; they must seek peace and pursue it. For the eyes of the Lord are on the righteous and his ears are attentive to their prayer, but the face of the Lord is against those who do evil.'" First I must keep my tongue from evil and my lips from deceitful speech. I am still in the starting blocks of the race for peace, and I can't seem to get past tongue problems. I've been tempted to create flavors for my feet (toe-paste) because I have put at least one foot in my mouth on so many occasions.

How do others address peace?

> Never be in a hurry; do everything quietly and in a calm spirit. Do not lose your inner peace for anything whatsoever, even if your whole world seems upset. (Saint Francis de Sales)[10]

> Those who are at war with others are not at peace with themselves. (William Hazlitt)[11]

> Lord, make me an instrument of thy peace. Where there is hatred, let me sow love. (Saint Francis of Assisi)[12]

My peace is frail and fleeting, and I find the message of 1 Peter 3:10–12 both very heartwarming to read and very difficult to follow. Perhaps I should follow my wife's humorous suggestion and use duct tape at every opportunity. Ouch! It is amazing how many disruptions of peace are created by careless words. It is difficult to say something wrong, if I would just be quiet. But sometimes the words just slip out. Pray for me, please!

Without a doubt, a warm smile is universally understood. If I see someone without a smile, I will give that person one of mine. I have plenty. The best example of peace I can give to others is to be at peace with myself. My prayer, heavenly Father, is, "Please direct me to that place of peace! In Jesus' name, amen!"

The fruit of the Spirit is peace!

Chapter 7

GPS of Forbearance or Patience

With emphasis on forbearance, let us read Galatians 5:22–23. "But the fruit of the Spirit is love, joy, peace, forbearance, kindness, goodness, faithfulness, gentleness and self-control. Against such things there is no law."

The purpose of the Holy Spirit's presence in the heart and life of a follower of Christ is to help us grow and mature and soar on wings of faith. We must continue to renew our efforts to be more like Christ in thought, in words, in deeds, in habits, in character, and in life.

What is forbearance or patience? It is the ability to endure and remain steadfast. Here are some great thoughts on patience.

> Have patience with all things, but, first of all
> with yourself. (Saint Francis de Sales)[13]

Great works are performed not by strength but
by perseverance.
(Samuel Johnson)[14]

Patience and perseverance have a magical effect
before which difficulties disappear and obstacles
vanish.
(John Quincy Adams)[15]

What causes me to lose my patience? Her is just a short list.

Why do I hate to wait? Do I always get in the shortest and fastest line at the grocery store?
Of course not!

What about instant gratification, instant results, instant relief, and instant justice? Even texting has to be done immediately despite safety concerns. If you are willing to pay more for shipping, your purchase can arrive in less time. Lack of patience can be costly.

What about inexcusable situations, irritations, inconveniences, and lack of competence by myself and others? It is amazing how often I am frustrated by traffic when I failed to allow enough time for the trip. It just may not be the other driver's fault that I have a problem. Let me recall when I was perfectly competent with everyone. Please keep on reading while I try to recall just one such day.

I am part of the *now* generation, and by that I mean that most of us want everything now. Have you ever watched a sales commercial that did not encourage impulse spending? Why are my expectations of my behavior so meager while I expect so much from others? Ouch!

Patience is the powerful attribute that enables a person to remain steadfast under trial or strain. A person who is tolerant and able to deal with a difficult person or situation without becoming angry demonstrates forbearance. What can I do to grow this fruit of the Spirit?

I must study and apply God's word, the true fountain of wisdom. Proverbs 19:11 reads, "A person's wisdom yields patience; it is to one's glory to overlook an offense."

Ephesians 4:2 recommends, "Be completely humble and gentle; be patient, bearing with one another in love." Asking a logical question of yourself or others can shift the conversation from emotion to logic. "Why is this happening?" is such a question. "Please help me understand!" is a humble request to address the concern logically.

Colossians 3:13 advises us, "Bear with each other and forgive one another if any of you has a grievance against someone. Forgive as the Lord forgave you." If it is to be, it is up to me! Please remember to forgive others and yourself in all things and then do what must be done for reconciliation if needed.

There is a very good reason why patience comes right after peace among the fruits of the Spirit. It is difficult to be angry or upset when I am at peace with myself and others. It is very difficult to be a good example to others when I am angry and upset. Other people may not remember what you said or did, but they will remember how you made them feel!

I literally push too hard for my own schedule and my own agenda. I definitely work better alone. I really try to be a team player, but why do others make that so difficult? Oops! I need to develop my patience. I can easily observe that I am not alone in this need. I must learn to be patient with myself first so I can go and do likewise with others.

I also need patience when I make important decisions. I should never make a decision when I am at a low point or in one of my worst moods. When impatient, I have made less than optimum decisions and later wished I had remembered that regret is not far away when I am impatient. Am I alone in this?

Most communication is basically nonverbal, so how did I behave when I was trying to be patient? When I am really upset, my ears become purple. Please, if you see me and my ears are purple, pray for me. What message am I communicating when my ears turn purple?

Patience is not only the ability to remain steadfast under trial and strain—it is also the ability to behave and not say something I will regret. On more than one occasion, I have been accused of not swimming in the deep end of the sensitivity pool. Maybe I should be the first person to buy this book. I bet you know a number of people who need to read this book as well.

We must learn to look to God. In Psalm 40:1, the psalmist wrote, "I waited patiently for the LORD; he turned to me and heard my cry."

"In His Time" is a beautiful song about waiting patiently on the Lord. I sang it many nights after I left my fully disabled mother in the long-term care facility. I do not understand, but I know our time on earth is short and heaven is waiting for followers of Christ. My mother was a follower. Thank you Father!

In Psalm 86:15, the psalmist wrote, "But you, Lord, are a compassionate and gracious God, slow to anger, abounding in love and faithfulness." Of all people, I must be truly thankful that God is slow to anger and abounding in love. I wish this for everyone.

In 2 Peter 3:9, the apostle wrote, "The Lord is not slow in keeping his promise, as some understand slowness. Instead he is patient with you, not wanting anyone to perish, but everyone to come to repentance." If I pray for opportunities to show God's love to others, the opportunities will come. Praying for these opportunities helps me to be more aware of others and their needs as well. Heavenly Father, help me to be an open door of your love for all. In Jesus' name, amen!

In Psalm 37:7a, the psalmist wrote, "Be still before the LORD and wait patiently for him." Jesus withdrew from others to be alone with God. If Jesus needed this communion with God, certainly I need more time with God in my life. Has Satan so filled our lives with so many activities that we are virtually never alone with God? This is a big red flag!

When I have Jesus Christ as the needle in my compass, I am learning to look to God. The entire book of John is truly reflective of what I should see as I walk on my spiritual journey. John has provided a unique insight into the life of Jesus Christ. John also said that Jesus did many other things that could have been written down as well. True followers of Christ are promised eternity with him. Oh heavenly Father, help me patiently and joyfully follow your Son with all my heart and soul. In Jesus' name, amen!

We must learn to emulate patient people. In Proverbs 15:18, we read, "A hot-tempered person stirs up conflict, but the one who is patient calms a quarrel." I can never have too many true followers of Christ in my life, but there is a real danger if I have too few. There is safety in numbers and this applies to going to church regularly. Gathering with the children of God should be on our weekly (not weakly) schedule.

The writer of Proverbs 22:24–25 has warned us about hot-tempered people. "Do not make friends with a hot-tempered person, do not associate with one easily angered, or you may learn their ways and get yourself ensnared." Again I should pray for God to bring people who fear and love God into my life. I should carefully interact with hot-tempered people.

The author of Hebrews 6:12 wrote, "We do not want you to become lazy, but to imitate those who through faith and patience inherit what has been promised." Tell others who are examples to you how much you admire their faith. Please always remember that you may be the only example of faith to some.

The author of Proverbs 14:29 wrote, "Whoever is patient has great understanding, but one who is quick-tempered displays folly." Remember that logical questions are effective transitions from emotional to logical thinking. Just ask open-ended questions to others and yourself.

From 1 Corinthians 10:13, we learn, "No temptation has overtaken you except what is common to mankind. And God is faithful; he will not let you be tempted beyond what you can bear. But when you are tempted, he will also provide a way out so that you can endure it." God will fulfill this promise every time I am tempted. I have no excuse, but I do have grace and mercy. Regardless of my failure, God will love me and will forgive me when I confess. Please never forget that God will never say "no" to a penitent Christian.

Romans 12:12 provides more encouragement. "Be joyful in hope, patient in affliction, faithful in prayer." I love to sing, and I love to listen to inspiring music. I love to feel good all the time, don't you?

As I consider patience, I am reminded of many times when I did not wait upon the Lord and implemented my own solutions to concerns in my life. In so many cases, my solutions were questionable, and the results were hard to bear. I was working in El Paso, Texas, and I knew that I would be relocated, but not when and where. Rather than pray and wait on the Lord, I actively pursued and found a solution in Irving, Texas. It turned out to be a financial and logistical nightmare that lingered for many years.

It is hard to accept that almost everything that is important takes time. God does not measure time as we do, and that concept is difficult for me to understand and apply. Joseph patiently waited on God for days that became weeks, for weeks that became months, and for months that became years. Meanwhile Joseph experienced injustice over and over while in captivity. When I review his pain, suffering, and patience, I feel ashamed. Truly I have been so blessed, and yet I find patience evasive. We should learn to praise God while he is stretching us.

Oh heavenly Father, gently lead me on the path to more patience. Help me to realize that I am so blessed and I need to show my gratitude through patience in all the areas of my life. In Jesus' name, amen!

The fruit of the Spirit is forbearance or patience!

CHAPTER 8

GPS of Kindness

Let us return, this time with emphasis on kindness, to Galatians 5:22–23: "But the fruit of the Spirit is love, joy, peace, forbearance, kindness, goodness, faithfulness, gentleness and self-control. Against such things there is no law."

The purpose of the Holy Spirit's presence in the heart and life of a follower of Christ is to help us grow and mature and soar on wings of faith. We must continue to renew our efforts to be more like Christ in thought, in words, in deeds, in habits, in character, and in life.

In our journey through life, we may meet some people only once. We have only one opportunity to make a first impression with everyone we meet as well. What do I want that first impression to be? What can I do to show others that I am kind?

A friendly smile is an act of kindness that everyone understands. Kind words can always bring some relief and cheer because everyone has concerns. One wonderful act of kindness is just being a good listener. God remembers every act of kindness—whether or not it is wanted or appreciated.

Each of us wishes for a better world in many ways, and acts of kindness are ways to make the world a better place. I need to look for ways to show kindness; I need to pray for ways to show kindness. If you pray sincerely, I know God will provide. So pray and get ready!

Others feel the same way as well!

> I shall pass through this world but once. Any good, therefore, that I can do or any kindness I can show to any human being, let me do it now. Let me not defer it or neglect it, for I shall not pass this way again. (Stephen Grellet)[16]

> Kind words do not cost much. Yet they accomplish much. (Blaise Pascal)[17]

> Kindness is the language which the deaf can hear and the blind can see. (Mark Twain)[18]

> Kindness in words creates confidence. Kindness in thinking creates profoundness. Kindness in giving creates love. (Lao Tzu)[19]

> No act of kindness, no matter how small, is ever wasted. (Aesop)[20]

How would you define kindness? Kindness is the ability to display friendly intent through words and deeds; it is also the will to improve another's well-being.

Kindness is the power to move close to another person in order to heal. Proverbs 12:25 emphasizes this power of kindness. "Anxiety weighs down the heart, but a kind word cheers it up."

Kindness is one's willingness to become involved in another's need. Scriptures affirm its necessity below.

Proverbs 14:31: "Whoever oppresses the poor shows contempt for their Maker, but whoever is kind to the needy honors God."

Romans 11:22: "Consider therefore the kindness and sternness of God: sternness to those who fell, but kindness to you, provided that you continue in his kindness. Otherwise, you also will be cut off."

Christians must be known for their kind hearts, kind words, and continual kind deeds. This is truly being a follower of Christ.

Ephesians 4:32 advised the early Christians on the practice of kindness. "Be kind and compassionate to one another, forgiving each other, just as in Christ God forgave you."

Colossians 3:12 also advised them on kindness. "Therefore, as God's chosen people, holy and dearly loved, clothe yourselves with compassion, kindness, humility, gentleness and patience."

Christian kindness is to be displayed even when its beneficiary does not want or appreciate it.

The applicability of kindness also receives emphasis in 2 Timothy 2:24: "And the Lord's servant must not be quarrelsome but must be kind to everyone, able to teach, not resentful."

Be mindful of the model God has shown us. God understands. As it is written in Hebrews 4:15, "For we do not have a high priest who is unable to empathize with our weaknesses, but we have one who has been tempted in every way, just as we are—yet he did not sin." I need to be able to address the weaknesses and needs of myself and others. I must have daily dialogue with someone who has been there—my Savior!

God is honest. Ephesians 4:14–15 emphasizes the virtue of candor. "Then we will no longer be infants, tossed back and forth by the waves, and blown here and there by every wind of teaching and by the cunning and craftiness of people in their deceitful scheming. Instead, speaking the truth in love, we will grow to become in every respect the mature body of him who is the head, that is, Christ."

Kindness is not blindness. We must care enough to confront others and ourselves. Honesty in relationships is essential in good times and bad ones. Jesus used care when confronting everyone with a spiritual need. He did not ignore a concern. *Caring for others in every concern* is the model he gave us.

God models forgiveness, as described in Romans 3:22–24. "This righteousness is given through faith in Jesus Christ to all who believe. There is no difference between Jew and Gentile, for all have sinned and fall short of the glory of God, and all are justified freely by his grace through the redemption that came by Christ Jesus." Whom do you need to forgive?

God affirms us in Romans 15:7: "Accept one another, then, just as Christ accepted you, in order to bring praise to God." Christ has accepted me as I am without any power or prestige. God is always thinking of us, and he gave his Son for us. We need to realize how important we are to God. Again, we need to fully comprehend how important we are to God.

God is spontaneous, as shown in Galatians 6:10. "Therefore, as we have opportunity, let us do good to all people, especially to those who belong to the family of believers." Kindness is love in action. Kindness is not passive.

Kindness is a choice. It cannot depend on how others relate to us. We all like to be around kind people, and almost all of us hate to see unkindness to others and to animals. Advertise how you feel about kindness by the way you live. Will I be a billboard for kindness today? If not, who will?

Simple, old-fashioned manners are acts of kindness as well— opening doors for others, letting other cars squeeze into your traffic lane, blessing sneezes, and other expressions of amity. Many words and phrases are wonderful acts of kindness— *please, thank you, after you, pardon me, have my seat,* and other expressions of politeness show kindness. I have not figured out exactly what is meant when others say *no problem, sounds like a plan,* or *it's all good.* So I relish the assurance that I was heard and someone was kind enough to respond.

I love the fact that random acts of kindness are receiving national attention—not for reward, but for everyone to become aware and look for spontaneous opportunities for kindness. Repayment of any act of kindness is wonderful but really not expected. The best way to repay an act of kindness is to pay it forward over and over. Starting right inside our homes, we all need a kinder world.

The fruit of the Spirit is kindness!

CHAPTER 9

GPS of Goodness

Galatians 5:22–23 also emphasized goodness. "But the fruit of the Spirit is love, joy, peace, forbearance, kindness, goodness, faithfulness, gentleness and self-control. Against such things there is no law."

The purpose of the Holy Spirit's presence in the heart and life of a follower of Christ is to help us grow and mature and soar on wings of faith. We must continue to renew our efforts to be more like Christ in thought, in words, in deeds, in habits, in character, and in life.

Goodness is an impossible commitment to being worthy of God. I am not worthy and will never be truly worthy, but I must aim high and must continue to mature my life in my Savior. God loves me as I am, but God wants me to grow.

It is interesting how others define goodness.

After the knowledge of, and obedience to, the will of God, the next aim must be to know something of His attributes of wisdom, power, and goodness as evidenced by His handiwork. (James Prescott Joule)[21]

Goodness is the only investment that never fails. (Henry David Thoreau)[22]

The fragrance of flowers spreads only in the direction of the wind. But the goodness of a person spreads in all directions. (Chanakya)[23]

To make one good action succeed another is the perfection of goodness.
(Ali ibn Abi Talib)[24]

What is goodness? Goodness is the absence of any unworthiness in my thoughts, in my words, in my deeds, in my habits, and in my character. Who can be perfectly good? I do not believe that "it's all good" is a realistic assessment of anything.

In Mark 10:18, Jesus addressed the issue of goodness. "Why do you call me good?" Jesus answered. "No one is good—except God alone." Goodness is one of the elements of the fruit of the Spirit, yet Jesus has told me that no one can be called good except God alone. Goodness is my goal, but perfecting it in my life on earth is not realistic. I will need to determine and enhance my understanding of goodness and what I need to do to allow goodness to permeate my life along with the other elements of the fruit of the Spirit.

Good versus Bad

In Matthew 6:22–23a, the apostle wrote, "The eye is the lamp of the body. If your eyes are healthy, your whole body will be full of light. But if your eyes are unhealthy, your whole body will be full of darkness." How do I actually see the world? Can you image a news broadcast or newspaper filled with only wonderful news? Unfortunately, I do not have to imagine news broadcasts filled with darkness. I have given up on dwelling in depth on news from any news outlet.

In Matthew 7:17–18, the apostle wrote, "Likewise, every good tree bears good fruit, but a bad tree bears bad fruit. A good tree cannot bear bad fruit, and a bad tree cannot bear good fruit." The bottom line is this. Was I able to provide living water to others through my spiritual fruit tempered with goodness? Did I help bring others closer to Christ?

There is another aspect to goodness. The seeming lack of badness does not necessarily imply the presence of goodness. In James 4:17, it is written, "If anyone, then, knows the good they ought to do and doesn't do it, it is sin for them." This is a very important concern for all followers: The omission of good and the commission of bad are both sins. I am convinced that sins of omission will prevent many Christian believers from becoming true followers of Christ. We must not hesitate to show the love of Christ at every opportunity.

Mindful of the Model

In Mark 10:17–18, we read, "As Jesus started on his way, a man ran up to him and fell on his knees before him. 'Good teacher,' he asked, 'what must I do to inherit eternal life?' 'Why do you call me good?' Jesus answered. 'No one is good—except God alone.'" Remember, God is our heavenly Father forever! So prayer is always a good option regardless. Our prayers are always heard and Jesus is our mediator. God has provided perfect communication whenever and wherever. Pray! Just do it!

In Acts 10:38, we can read "how God anointed Jesus of Nazareth with the Holy Spirit and power, and how he went around doing good and healing all who were under the power of the devil, because God was with him." Jesus was continually doing his Father's will. Jesus frequently left the crowds to be alone with God in thought and prayer and seek the Father's will. Perhaps this is the most important point of this book.

In Romans 8:28, we read, "And we know that in all things God works for the good of those who love him, who have been called according to his purpose." I am loved by God, and I have a purpose for my life. God was and is always there for me. If I am not close to God, it is totally my fault and shame.

In Ephesians 2:10 we read, "For we are God's handiwork, created in Christ Jesus to do good works, which God prepared in advance for us to do." God has given me a wonderful purpose for my life and the tools and the talents I need.

Living the Model

In Luke 6:27–36, we are instructed to be good regardless of the person or the situation. We are to love, do good, to bless, to pray, turn the other cheek, give up possessions lovingly, give freely, lend freely, and to be merciful. Why? Oh, what a promise is found in Luke 6:35b: "Then your reward will be great, and you will be children of the Most High."

Galatians 6:10 emphasizes positive behavior within the church. "Therefore, as we have opportunity, let us do good to all people, especially to those who belong to the family of believers." How much harm has been done by my being critical of members of my church family? Oh heavenly Father, please forgive me and make me whole! In Jesus' name, amen!

It is written in Titus 3:4–5a, "But when the kindness and love of God our Savior appeared, he saved us, not because of righteous things we had done, but because of his mercy." I think about the unmerciful servant in Matthew 18 and recall that God knows all. Mercy is another form of goodness. I desire grace and mercy—who can stand under truth and justice?

The takeaway lesson from all this discussion is that goodness must prevail in all I do. I have to look at my daily activities and see how I am doing at being actively good. I must be always mindful of the model. I must be living the model as well. God knows and will help. But I must seek his help in my prayers, and I must look for his guidance in my study of the Bible. And I can always use more quiet time with God to reflect on where I am and where God wants me to be.

The fruit of the Spirit is goodness!

Chapter 10

GPS of Faithfulness

This time with emphasis on faithfulness, we return to Galatians 5:22–23: "But the fruit of the Spirit is love, joy, peace, forbearance, kindness, goodness, faithfulness, gentleness and self-control. Against such things there is no law."

The purpose of the Holy Spirit's presence in the heart and life of a follower of Christ is to help us grow and mature and soar on wings of faith. We must continue to renew our efforts to be more like Christ in thought, in words, in deeds, in habits, in character, and in life.

Unfaithfulness is everywhere. One can see unfaithfulness in broken vows, outsourcing, biased news, disclaimers, and other current phenomena. Families and communities are being torn apart by broken vows, by companies relocating and outsourcing, biased news on people and events, and liability disclaimers. One of my personal favorites is a disclaimer located on the back of a lot of trucks that reads "Not responsible for broken windshields." As we see in the following scriptures, concerns about unfaithfulness are not new.

Psalm 12:1 contains the plea, "Help, LORD, for no one is faithful anymore; those who are loyal have vanished from the human race."

In Proverbs 20:6, we read, "Many claim to have unfailing love, but a faithful person who can find?"

In 2 Timothy 3:1–4, we read a warning. "But mark this: There will be terrible times in the last days. People will be lovers of themselves, lovers of money, boastful, proud, abusive, disobedient to their parents, ungrateful, unholy, without love, unforgiving, slanderous, without self-control, brutal, not lovers of the good, treacherous, rash, conceited, lovers of pleasure rather than lovers of God."

From these texts, I discern that a real concern about faithfulness has been around for a long time and will continue. I also discern that in the last days, there will be terrible times. Are we in the last days? Where is faithfulness to be found?

How do others see faithfulness?

> Nothing is more noble, nothing more venerable than fidelity. Faithfulness and truth are the most sacred excellences and endowments of the human mind. (Marcus Tullius Cicero)[25]

Endeavour to be faithful, and if there is any beauty in your thought, your style will be beautiful; if there is any real emotion to express, the expression will be moving. (George Henry Lewes)[26]

Faith is the virtue by which, clinging to the faithfulness of God, we lean upon him, so that we may obtain what he gives to us. (William Ames)[27]

How faithful is our God?

Scripture elaborates on God's faithfulness.

Psalm 89:2: "I will declare that your love stands firm forever, that you have established your faithfulness in heaven itself."

1 Corinthians 10:13b: "And God is faithful; he will not let you be tempted beyond what you can bear. But when you are tempted, he will also provide a way out so that you can endure it."

1 Peter 4:19: "So then, those who suffer according to God's will should commit themselves to their faithful Creator and continue to do good."

1 John 1:9: "If we confess our sins, he is faithful and just and will forgive us our sins and purify us from all unrighteousness."

Referring to the above texts, we can discern faithfulness as standing firm, persisting in doing good, remaining true to beliefs, and staying committed and loyal to our Creator. If I had to be faithful to one who is always faithful to me, our heavenly Father is the only choice.

How faithful am I?

Am I fully utilizing my God-given talents?

In Matthew 25:14–30 is a story of a faithful servant using his talents for his master. The talents were given out, those talents and more were received back, and the reward for faithfulness was bestowed on the faithful servant. Does God expect any less of me?

Can others rely on me even in the darkest of times? Scriptures address the issue of being reliability.

Proverbs 25:19: "Like a broken tooth or a lame foot is reliance on the unfaithful in a time of trouble." Trouble is more difficult to bear when I am alone.

Proverbs 17:17: "A friend loves at all times, and a brother is born for a time of adversity." Troubles are always lighter on extra shoulders. If you have a friend or friends like this, you are truly blessed. Thank God right now for your tried and true friends.

Am I financially responsible, using the 80-10-10 rule, in which 10 percent is for God, 10 percent is for savings, and 80 percent is for my living expenses? It is simplistic, but difficult to do for most of us.

Hebrews 13:5a contains advice on money—"Keep your lives free from the love of money and be content with what you have." I cannot focus on following Christ if I am focused on monetary concerns. Problems do not disappear for lottery winners or losers.

In 1 Timothy 6:10a, we are instructed, "For the love of money is a root of all kinds of evil." Oh, the endless grief that has been caused by money matters! Money should only be a tool to be used for the Lord, not the paramount desire in my life. I am certain that financial concerns have torn apart many marriages and destroyed many lives.

How much time is lost on worry and regret?

In Matthew 6:25 is found advice about worrying. "Therefore I tell you, do not worry about your life, what you will eat or drink; or about your body, what you will wear. Is not life more than food, and the body more than clothes?" Worry and regret are very poor investments of our time and energy.

If I were to make a list of everything I am worried about today, how accurate would my worry list be in 180 days? A lot of today's worries would just go away. Regret is one of Satan's ways to rob me of today. I still need to make the best of today in following Christ, not rehashing the past or stigmatizing the present.

> A day of worry is more exhausting than a week
> of work. (John Lubbock)[28]

God was there with me yesterday, God is here today, and God is already in my future. I need to learn to turn all my worries and regrets over to God in prayer. God will provide a way to ease my worries and resolve my regrets.

Am I committed to the three *W*s (whoever, whatever, and whenever) of service to God?

John 3:36: "**Whoever** believes in the Son has eternal life, but whoever rejects the Son will not see life, for God's wrath remains on them."

John 5:24: "Very truly I tell you, **whoever** hears my word and believes him who sent me has eternal life and will not be judged but has crossed over from death to life."

John 5:19b: "Very truly I tell you, the Son can do nothing by himself; he can do only what he sees his Father doing, because **whatever** the Father does the Son also does."

John 15:16: "You did not choose me, but I chose you and appointed you so that you might go and bear fruit—fruit that will last—and so that **whatever** you ask in my name the Father will give you."

One Corinthians 11:26: "For **whenever** you eat this bread and drink this cup, you proclaim the Lord's death until he comes."

Ephesians 6:19: "Pray also for me, that **whenever** I speak, words may be given me so that I will fearlessly make known the mystery of the gospel."

I am to be faithful at all times—when am I to bear fruit? I should bear the fruit of the Spirit with whoever is with me. I should bear the fruit of the Spirit in whatever environment or circumstance I encounter. I should bear the fruit of the Spirit whenever I can regardless. Am I committed to the three *W*s of service to God?

The fruit of the Spirit is faithfulness!

Chapter 11

GPS of Gentleness

To dwell upon gentleness, we revisit Galatians 5:22–23: "But the fruit of the Spirit is love, joy, peace, forbearance, kindness, goodness, faithfulness, gentleness and self-control. Against such things there is no law."

The purpose of the Holy Spirit's presence in the heart and life of a follower of Christ is to help us grow and mature and soar on wings of faith. We must continue to renew our efforts to be more like Christ in thought, in words, in deeds, in habits, in character, and in life.

Gentleness is a word that evokes a vision of a mother caring for her baby. Her words are soothing and reassuring. Her actions are deliberate and careful. Her hands are ever so soft and warm. A mother holding her baby is the very picture of gentleness.

Perhaps one of the greatest examples of gentleness is how Jesus Christ was so concerned about the little children. In Luke 18:15–17, we read, "People were also bringing babies to Jesus for him to place his hands on them. When the disciples saw this, they rebuked them. But Jesus called the children to him and said, 'Let the little children come to me, and do not hinder them, for the kingdom of God belongs to such as these. Truly I tell you, anyone who will not receive the kingdom of God like a little child will never enter it.'"

Am I still a child in my heart? I hope so!

We recognize gentleness in ourselves and others, and we are grateful for gentleness, especially when it is wanted and needed. We can also recognize the lack of gentleness. But how would you define gentleness? How have others defined it?

> A Christian reveals true humility by showing the gentleness of Christ, by being always ready to help others, by speaking kind words and performing unselfish acts, which elevate and ennoble the most sacred message that has come to our world. (Ellen G. White)[29]

> When you encounter difficulties and contradictions, do not try to break them, but bend them with gentleness and time. (Saint Francis De Sales)[30]

> Nothing is so strong as gentleness, nothing so gentle as real strength. (Saint Francis De Sales) [31]

Gentleness is the antidote for cruelty. (Phadrus)[32]

Gentleness corrects whatever is offensive in our manner. (Hugh Blair)[33]

Gentleness is marked by kindly words and deeds and accompanied by amiable and honorable behavior. Gentleness is real strength that is noble and refined.

I remember how gentle my mother was after my father had his debilitating stroke. He had been active eighteen hours a day for as long as I can remember and had seemed never to tire or get sick. Then he suffered a brain stem stroke. He became dependent on a wheelchair, and he developed a temper that seemed without mercy and without end.

But my mother weathered every storm with gentleness and selflessness. Her only concern was to give him every opportunity to embrace his new life with as much ease as possible. She sacrificed everything except her love and gentleness for him. Jessie Ruth Stepter was my mother and a follower of Christ all her life. I will always have her example of gentleness. She is one more reason why I want to go to heaven!

God's Words on Gentleness

Matthew 11:29: "Take my yoke upon you and learn from me, for I am gentle and humble in heart, and you will find rest for your souls."

Ephesians 4:2: "Be completely humble and gentle; be patient, bearing with one another in love."

Philippians 4:5: "Let your gentleness be evident to all. The Lord is near."

Colossians 3:12: "Therefore, as God's chosen people, holy and dearly loved, clothe yourselves with compassion, kindness, humility, gentleness and patience."

1 Peter 3:4: "Instead, it should be that of your inner self, the unfading beauty of a gentle and quiet spirit, which is of great worth in God's sight."

1 Peter 3:15–16: "But in your hearts set apart Christ as Lord. Always be prepared to give an answer to everyone who asks you to give the reason for the hope that you have. But do this with gentleness and respect, keeping a clear conscience, so that those who speak maliciously against your good behavior in Christ may be ashamed of their slander."

Gentleness is a supernatural gift that we can choose to accept. Gentle souls are not weak; they are gracious. They are not fierce but merciful. Gentle souls refuse to throw their weight around. Gentle souls treat people with courtesy and genuine concern.

This description of gentle behavior is very easy to believe, but it is very difficult to emulate. Driving in traffic is such a good indication of the posture of my soul. Traffic is challenging, and drivers deal with many distractions, including too many electronic devices. Gentleness and safety must be paramount while driving.

Gentleness—Life Applications

1. We are to be understanding but not demanding. As written in Philippians 2:3, "Do nothing out of selfish ambition or vain conceit, but in humility consider others better than yourselves." In a situation of power or control, how do you behave? Observing my behavior to waiters, custodians, and cashiers is one good way to evaluate my gentleness.

2. We are to be forgivers, not judges. Proverbs 17:9: "He who covers over an offense promotes love, but whoever repeats the matter separates close friends." How do you treat someone who disappoints you?

3. We are to be tender without surrender. As written in Proverbs 15:1, "A gentle answer turns away wrath, but a harsh word stirs up anger." How do you respond to your children when they are being offensive? I hope you do better than I did! We even attended a seminar on raising teenagers. It was still tough!

4. We are to be teachable, not unreachable. As the writer advises in James 1:19–20, "My dear brothers, take note of this: Everyone should be quick to listen, slow to speak and slow to become angry, for man's anger does not bring about the righteous life that God desires." How do you respond to people who correct you?

Gentleness is the best response to every situation. Gentleness is strength under control.

In Isaiah 42:2–4a, we read, "He will not shout or cry out, or raise his voice in the streets. A bruised reed he will not break, and a smoldering wick he will not snuff out. In faithfulness he will bring forth justice; he will not falter or be discouraged till he establishes justice on earth."

The fruit of the Spirit is gentleness!

CHAPTER 12

GPS of Self-control

Returning to Galatians 5:22–23, we now focus on self-control. "But the fruit of the Spirit is love, joy, peace, forbearance, kindness, goodness, faithfulness, gentleness and self-control. Against such things there is no law."

The purpose of the Holy Spirit's presence in the heart and life of a follower of Christ is to help us grow and mature and soar on wings of faith. We must continue to renew our efforts to be more like Christ in thought, in words, in deeds, in habits, in character, and in life.

In 2 Timothy 3:1–4, there is a warning. "But mark this: There will be terrible times in the last days. People will be lovers of themselves, lovers of money, boastful, proud, abusive, disobedient to their parents, ungrateful, unholy, without love, unforgiving, slanderous, without self-control, brutal, not lovers of the good, treacherous, rash, conceited, lovers of pleasure rather than lovers of God."

Is there any doubt that we live in such an alarming time? Am I part of the problem? Am I part of the solution?

How can I truly evaluate the amount of self-control in my life? Listed here are some manifestations of the lack of self-control.

- credit card debt
- instant gratification
- supersizing
- immodesty in public
- making bad choices
- shallow song lyrics
- a slave to electronic devices
- watching horrific entertainment
- political correctness to a fault
- too many reactive decisions

To show the self-control as a follower of Christ, I must let Christ help me give meaning and purpose to everything I say and do. I should plan to be proactive, not reactive. Why is self-control an element of the fruit of the Spirit?

> But what is liberty without wisdom, and without
> virtue? It is the greatest of all possible evils; for
> it is folly, vice, and madness, without tuition or
> restraint. (Edmund Burke)[34]

Liberty exists in proportion to wholesome
restraint. (Daniel Webster)[35]

Do not bite at the bait of pleasure till you know
there is no hook beneath it.
(Thomas Jefferson)[36]

The test of good manners is to be patient with
the bad ones. (Solomon Ibn Gabirol)[37]

Our God wants us to be disciplined and controlled. Why?

In 2 Peter 1:5–8, the apostle wrote, "For this very reason, make every
effort to add to your faith goodness; and to goodness, knowledge;
and to knowledge, self-control; and to self-control, perseverance;
and to perseverance, Godliness; and to Godliness, mutual affection;
and to mutual affection, love. For if you possess these qualities in
increasing measure, they will keep you from being ineffective and
unproductive in your knowledge of our Lord Jesus Christ."

Peter emphasized a number of the elements of the fruit of the Spirit
and other elements as well. He pointed out that faith is not blind and
that knowledge is critical. I must be fully aware that I am a child of
God and why. If I am not sure, then more Bible study is needed. We
should study daily—certainly not just weekly or weakly.

The power from above that is all around us and in us is the Holy Spirit.

Galatians 5:16 emphasizes self-control and deliberation. "So I
say, walk by the Spirit, and you will not gratify the desires of the

flesh." God gives us the power to make responsible long-term and eternal decisions. He also provides us with the ability to plan proactive decisions for future choices.

<u>He protects us from overwhelming temptation. How?</u>

In 1 Corinthians 10:13, we read, "No temptation has overtaken you except what is common to mankind. And God is faithful; he will not let you be tempted beyond what you can bear. But when you are tempted, he will also provide a way out so that you can endure it." Navigate to islands of safety. Others have been tempted just like me, and God will help. Take a stand on God's promise.

> In matters of style swim with the current; in matters of principle, stand like a rock. (Thomas Jefferson)[38]

Galatians 6:9 suggests, "Let us not become weary in doing good, for at the proper time we will reap a harvest if we do not give up."

Proverbs 3:11–12 contains the familiar admonition, "My son, do not despise the LORD's discipline, and do not resent his rebuke, because the LORD disciplines those he loves, as a father the son he delights in." All followers of Christ have grace and mercy for the forgiveness of our sins, but we are not guaranteed protection from the consequences.

In Proverbs 25:28 we find a symbol: "Like a city whose walls are broken through is a person who lacks self-control." Self-control enables temperance, restraint, and self-discipline in our lives. Is this what I want and need?

Psalm 19:14 advises us, "May these words of my mouth and this meditation of my heart be pleasing in your sight, LORD, my Rock and my Redeemer." This should be true even when driving in traffic.

From Philippians 4:8 we can receive wise counsel on directing our thoughts: "Finally, brothers and sisters, whatever is true, whatever is noble, whatever is right, whatever is pure, whatever is lovely, whatever is admirable—if anything is excellent or praiseworthy—think about such things." So much of who we are is determined by our thoughts. This one verse helps me easily realize how my frame of mind should be. But having this mindset is so very difficult to achieve and maintain without help.

A self-control starter kit begins with the word self. We must clean up our act according to the advice in Luke 6:41: "Why do you look at the speck of sawdust in your brother's eye and pay no attention to the plank in your own eye?"

Collateral damage from the lack of self-control may take a while to correct and cleanup. Some of the damage may be beyond recovery. But do what you can and leave the rest to God. God will provide. Peter made three bad denials in one night, but he turned back to God, and Jesus reinstated Peter. Judas did not turn back to God. What about me? How do I regain my self-control and recover from the consequences?

Start with seeking out the truth about where you are and how you got there. Ask God in prayer, in thought, in conversation to show you where you are and how you got there.

Here is my take on why self-control is very difficult for me. For some reason, everything has to make sense and be logical in my small corner of the world. I see what ought to be and ought to happen. My expectations for others and myself are very realistic to me.

I have prayed all my life to have a wonderful relationship with my Dad. If we were together too long, our relationship would be strained. I thought I had realistic expectations for each of us and I would eventually leave disappointed.

He and I had a discussion one afternoon about lowering our personal expectations and focus on being glad we are together. God answered my prayers and when we were together, each of us was blessed by it.

Before those times, it was tough being around my Dad. He could say things that hurt deeply. I, too, have said things to family and others that hurt deeply. I have failed to really comprehend that what I say and do affects others. Sometimes, the best thing to say or do is nothing, just let it go. Shame on me!

Self-control is the last of the nine elements for a purpose. My testimony is worthless without self-control. People may not remember what I say or do, but they will remember how I made them feel. Am I a positive example – a follower of Christ? Am I fully under the control of the Holy Spirit? No, but I need to keep on trying!

The fruit of the Spirit is self-control!

CHAPTER 13

Against Such Things There Is No Law

With emphasis on its conclusion this time, we review Galatians 5:22–23. "But the fruit of the Spirit is love, joy, peace, forbearance, kindness, goodness, faithfulness, gentleness and self-control. Against such things there is no law."

Here are some interesting observations about Galatians 5:22–23.

All expressions are positive.

All expressions are unselfish.

All expressions are focused on relationships.

A summary of each fruit of the Spirit:

- **Love** is the ability to seek the good of others, regardless of the sacrifice.

- **Joy** is an inner satisfaction and sense of delight that comes to you in the knowledge of a secure relationship with God.
- **Peace** is the ability to live in serenity with God, self, and others.
- **Patience** is the power to deal with people and circumstances until God brings his own good purposes to light in them.
- **Kindness** is a willingness to be involved in another person's needs in order to help meet their needs.
- **Goodness** is upright and honorable conduct tempered by a generosity and a charitable spirit.
- **Faithfulness** is the quality of utter dependability, reliability, and loyalty.
- **Gentleness** is strength under divine control.
- **Self-control** is the power to restrain the forces and appetites that could enslave, harm, or ruin me.

Here is how my wife and I presented the fruit of the Spirit to the staff where she worked as a registered nurse for several years. She retired to watch our three-year-old grandson.

- I wish you **love** for each other as you labor hard together to provide critical medical care to the Dallas-Fort Worth area.
- I wish you **joy** as you, in your way, improve the quality of life for so many patients.
- I wish you **peace** at the end of each day, knowing you have done a great service for those in need.

- I wish you **patience** with each other, knowing that sometimes all of you are overwhelmed.
- I wish you **kindness** in all that you say and do. Your smile is like a candle that brings not only light but warmth.
- I wish you **goodness** in life so that the past is a pleasant memory and your days are truly blessed.
- I wish you **faithfulness** to God, our Father, as all our services are truly for him.
- I wish you **gentleness** in dealing with each other. Others will remember how you made them feel for a long time.
- I wish you **self-control** so that you can live every day without regret.

I should wish these for all people in my work, in my church family, in my home, and all through my life. If you made a wish list for others that you have come to know and love what would it contain? Seriously, what would you list? If this is a wake-up call for you and me, then we need the GPS from above to bring us back in step with Jesus Christ.

The basic requirements of a spirit-filled life are

1. daily awareness of my weaknesses and vulnerability to sin;
2. daily renewal of my commitment to the Lordship of Jesus;
3. daily repentance relative to the passions and desires of my sinful nature; and

4. daily choosing to grow the fruit of the Spirit of God and follow Jesus.

   You should examine yourself daily. If you find faults, you should correct them. When you find none, you should try even harder. (Anonymous)[39]

   What lies behind us and what lies before us are tiny matters compared to what lies within us. (Ralph Waldo Emerson)[40]

   Preach the Gospel at all times, and when necessary use words. (Anonymous)[41]

As I live as a follower of Christ, I will not walk the straight and narrow path without allowing Jesus Christ to be the needle in my compass. The fruit of the Spirit provides nine essential elements that I can measure and grow my becoming more like Christ. I need have no concern about their relevance in my life as a follower of Christ.

Against such things there is no law!

CHAPTER 14

Observations from My Journey

Life is full of bubbles that pop up seemingly out of nowhere and can affect us for a moment or for a lifetime. Bubbles are anything that affects the status quo of our daily lives and routines. Bubbles can be expected or not. They can be any number of activities or happenings that come our way and require our action. Some may be welcome and some may not. There are many bubbles in all our lives.

How we react to these bubbles can help determine where we are in our walk with God. Some bubbles change us for an instant, some for a lifetime, and some forever. If we are to prevail to the end of our earthly journey, we will need God's powerful Spirit lifting us from the condition of a spiritual gooney bird that struggles on earth to that of a spiritual albatross that soars above.

It is hard to focus on what is really important when I am drowning in too many bubbles, regardless of their importance. Bubbles can bury any and all achievement under a mountain of unproductive activity.

In the 1960s, computers were initially designed to save time and shorten the workweek. Computers were to take on mundane tasks and allow us to focus on more important tasks. Since then, we may have lost our way.

Word-processing applications have generated additional mounds of paperwork—for example, the forms needed to buy or sell anything of substantial value. Spreadsheet applications have provided the ability to overanalyze data and have taken micromanagement to a unique dimension.

Also, in the computer age, we have bumped up our priorities. We have seen normal priorities become important, important priorities become urgent, urgent priorities become critical, and critical priorities become a matter of life and death. When did the wheels fall off?

Too many bubbles at the bottom of a waterfall can be a life-threatening trap even for an experienced swimmer. Too many bubbles from the commitments in my life can become a spiritually deadly trap in which I am literally too busy to be a very good Christian. Have I confused activity with achievement? Have you?

How can I ever hope to minimize the bubbles in my life? What have I done just this week that has eternal importance?

I know I cannot eliminate all the bubbles—so many are not under my control or of my choosing. Where did all these bubbles come from? Was there a return address on the bubble when it arrived? I wish there were.

I need to remember that it took a while for me to get buried in bubbles, and it will take a while to recover and gain control and become proactive again. Let's make a list of possible manageable sources of bubbles.

- Not being unable to say *no* without feeling guilty. Matthew 5:37 provides guidance on this point: "All you need to say is simply 'Yes' or 'No'; anything beyond this comes from the evil one."
- Not checking with my spouse first.
- Not want to disappoint others and agreeing for the wrong reasons.
- Contending with too much information and talking myself into trouble.
- Sins that we commit willingly. These can become big bubble generators.
- Sins of omission that involve the failure to do right, because my conscience is ever with me. In James 4:17, the writer wrote, "If anyone, then, knows the good they ought to do and doesn't do it, it is sin for them."

- There is letting others say *yes* for me when I have the choice. I must remember that no commitment is too big when someone else chooses it for me.
- There is too much negative speech to myself and others.
- There is failure to attend important seminars on marriage, raising teenagers, and other important topics.

It is amazing how children can fill our lives with ongoing commitments to so many high-priority activities. Dare we forget the grandchildren? And one day, whether they or we realize it or not, our parents will need us. Between the wants and needs of our parents and those of our children is a zone of time pressure that creates an endless supply of bubbles. Now my spouse's parents and mine are gone, and our children are grown. We are blessed with four grandsons and a granddaughter, who is in heaven. I do not know how we could have made it through all the bubbles without Jesus Christ as our Lord and Savior.

Dear heavenly Father, thank you for my wonderful wife and our wonderful family of three daughters and one son. And thank you for our extended family through marriage. Thank you for our four grandsons and our granddaughter, whose days with us were too few. Thank you for our wonderful parents. Thank you for all of the really important bubbles that tied our lives together forever. In Jesus' name, amen!

CHAPTER 15

Lukewarm: Neither Cold nor Hot

Revelations 3:15–17 contains a famous accusation—"I know your deeds, that you are neither cold nor hot. I wish you were either one or the other! So, because you are lukewarm—neither hot nor cold—I am about to spit you out of my mouth. You say, 'I am rich; I have acquired wealth and do not need a thing.' But you do not realize that you are wretched, pitiful, poor, blind and naked."

> The immortality of the soul is a matter which is of so great consequence to us and which touches us so profoundly that we must have lost all feeling to be indifferent about it. (Blaise Pascal)[42]

> The sensitivity of men to small matters, and their indifference to great ones, indicates a strange inversion. (Blaise Pascal)[43]

Well stated! It is amazing how the devil can divert our focus from important eternal matters. We can become lukewarm if we lose our sense of direction and purpose. If I wanted to gauge my temperature as a Christian, what would I check?

1. Do I worship weekly with other Christians?
2. Do I share fellowship with other Christians?
3. Am I so politically correct that I deny Christ?
4. Do I use religion as a weapon?
5. Am I a faultfinder?
6. Do I gossip?
7. Am I reading this list and thinking only of others?

Unfortunately for me, one could pick a number—any number! I could have been drafted into the army of lukewarm Christians for any and all of the above concerns during my earthly journey. And if I am not steadfast as a Christian, I could be drafted anywhere, at any time. I mean it! I fail so miserably at times that I am too ashamed to go to God in prayer and ask for grace and mercy.

Why am I continually the victim when I should be the victor as a follower of Christ? Why do I even consider not going to God in prayer? Have I ever really been worthy to go before God in prayer? Only through the blood of Jesus!

There is really good news in Revelations 3:19: "Those whom I love I rebuke and discipline. So be earnest and repent." We may become lukewarm from time to time, but God loves us regardless and wants us back under his control and guidance—the GPS from above can help determine our temperature and help us find our way back to being Christians on fire for the Lord.

CHAPTER 16

In Summary

The purpose of the Spirit's presence in the heart and life of a follower of Christ is to produce Christ like character. We must continue to renew our efforts to be Christ like in thought, in words, in deeds, in habits, in character, and in life.

There are very few real heroes in our lives. Other than the heroes of the Bible, my personal hero is John Wayne. He was truly bigger than life. However, the list of faithful people of God in Hebrews 11 is very humbling to me. If I scrutinize their lives, I will find the fruit of the Spirit. If I scrutinize my life, I need to kneel and beg for grace and mercy, not truth and justice.

I have tried not to detract or subtract from the word of God when I added some of my personal thoughts on the Bible scriptures and the other materials presented here. I have tried to let the spiritual truths of God's words—the living water—pour through me freely and purely. Who am I?

"Who am I?" is a great question that all of us need to ask. This book contains many open-ended questions that I must ask myself and that you, I hope, will ask yourself. I am and always will be a work in progress on my earthly journey, and I hope and pray that the wings of the Holy Spirit—the GPS from above—will allow me to be an albatross on many occasions. God bless you and yours. I leave you with this beautiful scriptural text that conveys life as a follower of Christ.

> Rejoice in the Lord always. I will say it again: Rejoice! Let your gentleness be evident to all. The Lord is near. Do not be anxious about anything, but in every situation, by prayer and petition, with thanksgiving, present your requests to God. And the peace of God, which transcends all understanding, will guard your hearts and your minds in Christ Jesus. Finally, brothers and sisters, whatever is true, whatever is noble, whatever is right, whatever is pure, whatever is lovely, whatever is admirable—if anything is excellent or praiseworthy—think about such things. Whatever you have learned or received or heard from me, or seen in me—put it into practice. And the God of peace will be with you. (Philippians 4:4–9)

New International Version Bible References Listed by Chapter

Preface

- Galatians 5:22–23
- John 17:20–23

Chapter 1
Introduction

- 1 John 2:16
- Luke 12:6
- John 14:6
- Galatians 5:22–23
- John 1:46

Chapter 2
Where Do I Begin?

- John 14:6
- John 14:16–17
- John 14:23
- Psalm 119:105
- Romans 7:14–15
- Titus 3:4–7

Chapter 3
What Must I Do Today?

- Matthew 15:18–19
- Galatians 5:22–23
- Galatians 5:19–20
- Romans 8:1–2
- Galatians 5:22–23

Chapter 4
GPS of Love

- Galatians 5:22–23
- Hebrews 3:1
- Matthew 22:37–39
- Colossians 3:14
- 1 Corinthians 13:1–3
- 1 Corinthians 13:4–8a
- John 3:16
- Luke 6:31

- Matthew 5:43–45a
- Matthew 5:3–10

Chapter 5
GPS of Joy

- Galatians 5:22–23
- Romans 12:9
- James 3:16
- Hebrews 12:15
- 1 John 4:18a
- Acts 20:35b
- John 3:16
- Colossians 3:13
- Psalms 62:8
- Philippians 4:4
- Philippians 4:13

Chapter 6
GPS of Peace

- Galatians 5:22–23
- 1 John 2:16
- 1 Peter 5:8
- Matthew 6:31–32
- John 16:33
- John 14:27
- Luke 10:41–42
- Romans 5:1
- Colossians 1:20

- Colossians 3:15a
- Philippians 4:6–7
- Romans 12:18
- Hebrews 12:14
- Ephesians 4:3
- Matthew 5:24
- 2 Corinthians 5:18
- 1 Peter 3:10–12

Chapter 7
GPS of Forbearance or Patience

- Galatians 5:22–23
- Proverbs 19:11
- Ephesians 4:2
- Colossians 3:13
- Proverbs 19:11
- Psalms 40:1
- Psalms 86:15
- 2 Peter 3:9
- Psalms 37:7a
- Proverbs 15:18
- Proverbs 22:24–25
- Hebrews 6:12
- Proverbs 14:29
- 1 Corinthians 10:13
- Romans 12:12

Chapter 8
GPS of Kindness

- Galatians 5:22–23
- Proverbs 12:25
- Proverbs 14:31
- Romans 11:22
- Ephesians 4:32
- Colossians 3:12
- 2 Timothy 2:24
- Hebrews 4:15
- Ephesians 4:14–15
- Romans 3:22–24
- Romans 15:7
- Galatians 6:10

Chapter 9
GPS of Goodness

- Galatians 5:22–23
- Mark 10:18
- Matthew 6:22–23a
- Matthew 7:17–18
- James 4:17
- Mark 10:17–18
- Acts 10:38
- Romans 8:28
- Ephesians 2:10
- Luke 6:27–36
- Luke 6:35b

- Galatians 6:10
- Titus 3:4–5a

Chapter 10
GPS of Faithfulness

- Galatians 5:22–23
- Psalms 12:1
- Proverbs 20:6
- 2 Timothy 3:1–4
- Psalms 89:2
- 1 Corinthians 10:13b
- 1 Peter 4:19
- 1 John 1:9
- Matthew 25:14–30
- Proverbs 25:19
- Proverbs 17:17
- Hebrews 13:5a
- 1 Timothy 6:10
- Matthew 6:25
- John 3:36
- John 5:24
- John 5:19
- John 15:16
- 1 Corinthians 11:26
- Ephesians 6:19

Chapter 11
GPS of Gentleness

- Galatians 5:22–23
- Matthew 11:29
- Ephesians 4:2
- Philippians 4:5
- Colossians 3:12
- 1 Peter 3:4
- 1 Peter 3:15–16
- Philippians 2:3
- Proverbs 17:9
- Proverbs 15:1
- James 1:19–20
- Isaiah 42:2–4a

Chapter 12
GPS of Self-control

- Galatians 5:22–23
- 2 Timothy 3:1–4
- 2 Peter 1:5–8
- Galatians 5:16
- 1 Corinthians 10:13
- Galatians 6:9
- Proverbs 3:11–12
- Proverbs 25:28
- Psalms 19:14
- Philippians 4:8
- Luke 6:41

Chapter 13
"Against such things there is no law."

- Galatians 5:22–23

Chapter 14
Observations from My Journey

- Matthew 5:37
- James 4:17

Chapter 15
Lukewarm: Neither Cold nor Hot

- Revelations 3:15–17
- Revelations 3:19

Chapter 16
In Summary

- Philippians 4:4–9

CITATIONS

1. Henry David Thoreau, BrainyQuote.com, Xplore Inc., accessed June 13, 2016, http://www.brainyquote.com/quotes/quotes/h/henrydavid121510.html.

2. Ralph Waldo Emerson, BrainyQuote.com, Xplore Inc., accessed June 13, 2016, http://www.brainyquote.com/quotes/quotes/r/ralphwaldo103408.html.

3. Thomas Jefferson, BrainyQuote.com, Xplore Inc., accessed June 13, 2016, http://www.brainyquote.com/quotes/quotes/t/thomasjeff133143.html.

4. Lao Tzu, BrainyQuote.com, Xplore Inc., accessed June 13, 2016, http://www.brainyquote.com/quotes/quotes/l/laotzu101043.html.

5. Saint Francis of Assisi, BrainyQuote.com, Xplore Inc., accessed June 13, 2016, http://www.brainyquote.com/quotes/quotes/f/francisofa153348.html.

6. Oscar Wilde, BrainyQuote.com, Xplore Inc., accessed June 13, 2016, http://www.brainyquote.com/quotes/quotes/o/oscarwilde121811.html.

7. Tecumseh, BrainyQuote.com, Xplore Inc., accessed June 13, 2016, http://www.brainyquote.com/quotes/quotes/t/tecumseh190018.html.

8. Marcus Tullius Cicero, BrainyQuote.com, Xplore Inc., accessed June 13, 2016, http://www.brainyquote.com/quotes/quotes/m/marcustull130785.html.

9. Hosea Ballou, BrainyQuote.com, Xplore Inc., accessed June 13, 2016, http://www.brainyquote.com/quotes/quotes/h/hoseaballo149578.html.

10. Saint Francis de Sales, BrainyQuote.com, Xplore Inc., accessed June 13, 2016, http://www.brainyquote.com/quotes/quotes/s/saintfranc131350.html.

11. William Hazlitt, BrainyQuote.com, Xplore Inc., accessed June 13, 2016, http://www.brainyquote.com/quotes/quotes/w/williamhaz383510.html.

12. Saint Francis of Assisi, BrainyQuote.com, Xplore Inc., accessed June 13, 2016, http://www.brainyquote.com/quotes/quotes/f/francisofa389169.html.

13. Saint Francis de Sales, BrainyQuote.com, Xplore Inc., accessed June 13, 2016, http://www.brainyquote.com/quotes/quotes/s/saintfranc193306.html.

14. Samuel Johnson, BrainyQuote.com, Xplore Inc., accessed June 13, 2016, http://www.brainyquote.com/quotes/quotes/s/samueljohn121919.html.

15. John Quincy Adams, BrainyQuote.com, Xplore Inc., accessed June 13, 2016, http://www.brainyquote.com/quotes/quotes/j/johnquincy387094.html.

16. Stephen Grellet, BrainyQuote.com, Xplore Inc., accessed June 13, 2016, http://www.brainyquote.com/quotes/quotes/s/stephengre651572.html.

17. Blaise Pascal, BrainyQuote.com, Xplore Inc., accessed June 13, 2016, http://www.brainyquote.com/quotes/quotes/b/blaisepasc159858.html.

18. Mark Twain, BrainyQuote.com, Xplore Inc., accessed June 13, 2016, http://www.brainyquote.com/quotes/quotes/m/marktwain106287.html.

19. Lao Tzu, BrainyQuote.com, Xplore Inc., accessed June 13, 2016, http://www.brainyquote.com/quotes/quotes/l/laotzu118352.html.

20. Aesop, BrainyQuote.com, Xplore Inc., accessed June 13, 2016, http://www.brainyquote.com/quotes/quotes/a/aesop109734.html.

21. James Prescott Joule, BrainyQuote.com, Xplore Inc., accessed June 13, 2016, http://www.brainyquote.com/quotes/quotes/j/jamespresc317814.html.

22. Henry David Thoreau, BrainyQuote.com, Xplore Inc., accessed June 13, 2016, http://www.brainyquote.com/quotes/quotes/h/henrydavid106122.html.

23. Chanakya, BrainyQuote.com, Xplore Inc., accessed June 13, 2016, http://www.brainyquote.com/quotes/quotes/c/chanakya201071.html.

24. Ali Ibn Abi Talib, BrainyQuote.com, Xplore Inc., accessed June 13, 2016, http://www.brainyquote.com/quotes/quotes/a/aliibnabit201056.html.

25. Marcus Tullius Cicero, BrainyQuote.com, Xplore Inc., accessed June 13, 2016, http://www.brainyquote.com/quotes/quotes/m/marcustull133288.html.

26. George Henry Lewes, BrainyQuote.com, Xplore Inc., accessed June 13, 2016, http://www.brainyquote.com/quotes/quotes/g/georgehenr287490.html.

27. William Ames, BrainyQuote.com, Xplore Inc., accessed June 13, 2016, http://www.brainyquote.com/quotes/quotes/w/williamame301276.html.

28. John Lubbock, BrainyQuote.com, Xplore Inc., accessed June 13, 2016, http://www.brainyquote.com/quotes/quotes/j/johnlubboc122326.html.

29. Ellen G. White, BrainyQuote.com, Xplore Inc., accessed June 13, 2016, http://www.brainyquote.com/quotes/quotes/e/ellengwhi533089.html.

30. Saint Francis de Sales, BrainyQuote.com, Xplore Inc., accessed June 13, 2016, http://www.brainyquote.com/quotes/quotes/s/saintfranc143989.html.

31. Saint Francis de Sales, BrainyQuote.com, Xplore Inc., accessed June 13, 2016, http://www.brainyquote.com/quotes/quotes/s/saintfranc193305.html.

32. Phaedrus, BrainyQuote.com, Xplore Inc., accessed June 13, 2016, http://www.brainyquote.com/quotes/quotes/p/phaedrus176318.html.

33. Hugh Blair, BrainyQuote.com, Xplore Inc., accessed June 13, 2016, http://www.brainyquote.com/quotes/quotes/h/hughblair192618.html.

34. Edmund Burke, BrainyQuote.com, Xplore Inc., accessed June 13, 2016, http://www.brainyquote.com/quotes/quotes/e/edmundburk402383.html.

35. Daniel Webster, BrainyQuote.com, Xplore Inc., accessed June 13, 2016, http://www.brainyquote.com/quotes/quotes/d/danielwebs118447.html.

36. Thomas Jefferson, BrainyQuote.com, Xplore Inc., accessed June 13, 2016, http://www.brainyquote.com/quotes/quotes/t/thomasjeff157235.html.

37. Solomon Ibn Gabirol, BrainyQuote.com, Xplore Inc., accessed June 13, 2016, http://www.brainyquote.com/quotes/quotes/s/solomonibn164759.html.

38. Thomas Jefferson, BrainyQuote.com, Xplore Inc., accessed June 13, 2016, http://www.brainyquote.com/quotes/quotes/t/thomasjeff121032.html.

39. Unknown, BrainyQuote.com, Xplore Inc., accessed June 13, 2016, http://www.brainyquote.com/quotes/quotes/u/unknown145096.html.

40. Ralph Waldo Emerson, BrainyQuote.com, Xplore Inc., accessed June 13, 2016, http://www.brainyquote.com/quotes/quotes/r/ralphwaldo386697.html.

41. Unknown, BrainyQuote.com, Xplore Inc., accessed June 13, 2016, http://www.brainyquote.com/quotes/quotes/u/unknown109569.html.

42. Blaise Pascal, BrainyQuote.com, Xplore Inc., accessed June 13, 2016, http://www.brainyquote.com/quotes/quotes/b/blaisepasc402149.html.

43. Blaise Pascal, BrainyQuote.com, Xplore Inc., accessed June 13, 2016, http://www.brainyquote.com/quotes/quotes/b/blaisepasc401010.html.